ECCLESIASTES

DISCOVER TOGETHER BIBLE STUDY SERIES

1 Peter: Discovering Encouragement in Troubling Times
1 Timothy: Discovering Clarity in a World That Can't Agree
1 and 2 Thessalonians: Discovering Hope in a Promised Future
Daniel: Discovering the Courage to Stand for Your Faith
Ecclesiastes: Discovering Meaning in a Meaningless World
Ephesians: Discovering Your Identity and Purpose in Christ
Galatians: Discovering Freedom in Christ Through Daily Practice
Hosea: Discovering God's Fierce Love
Isaiah: Discovering Assurance Through Prophecies About Your Mighty King
James: Discovering the Joy of Living Out Your Faith
Luke: Discovering Healing in Jesus's Words to Women
Philippians: Discovering Joy Through Relationship
Proverbs: Discovering Ancient Wisdom for a Postmodern World, Volume 1
Proverbs: Discovering Ancient Wisdom for a Postmodern World, Volume 2
Psalms: Discovering Authentic Worship
Revelation: Discovering Life for Today and Eternity
Ruth: Discovering God's Faithfulness in an Anxious World

Leader's guides are available at www.discovertogetherseries.com

ECCLESIASTES

Discovering Meaning in a Meaningless World

Sue Edwards

KREGEL
PUBLICATIONS

Ecclesiastes: Discovering Meaning in a Meaningless World
© 2018 by Sue Edwards

Published by Kregel Publications, a division of Kregel Inc., 2450 Oak Industrial Dr. NE, Grand Rapids, MI 49505.

ISBN 978-0-8254-4879-9

Printed in the United States of America

24 25 26 27 28 29 30 / 5 4 3 2 1

Contents

Contents

How to Get the Most Out of a Discover Together Bible Study

Women today need Bible study to keep balanced, focused, and Christ-centered in their busy worlds. The tiered questions in *Ecclesiastes: Discovering Meaning in a Meaningless World* allow you to choose a depth of study that fits your lifestyle, which may even vary from week to week, depending on your schedule.

Just completing the basic questions will require about one and a half hours per lesson, and will provide a basic overview of the text. For busy women, this level offers in-depth Bible study with a minimum time commitment.

"Digging Deeper" questions are for those who want to, and make time to, probe the text even more deeply. Answering these questions may require outside resources such as an atlas, Bible dictionary, or concordance; you may be asked to look up parallel passages for additional insight; or you may be encouraged to investigate the passage using an interlinear Greek-English text or *Vine's Expository Dictionary*. This deeper study will challenge you to learn more about the history, culture, and geography related to the Bible, and to grapple with complex theological issues and differing views. Some with teaching gifts and an interest in advanced academics will enjoy exploring the depths of a passage, and might even find themselves creating outlines and charts and writing essays worthy of seminarians!

This inductive Bible study is designed for both individual and group discovery. You will benefit most if you tackle each week's lesson on your own, and then meet with other women to share insights, struggles, and aha moments. Bible study leaders will find a free, downloadable leader's guide for each study, along with general tips for leading small groups, at www.discovertogetherseries.com.

Choose a realistic level of Bible study that fits your schedule. You may want to finish the basic questions first, and then "dig deeper" as time permits. Take time to savor the questions, and don't rush through the application. Read the sidebars for additional insight to enrich the experience. Note the optional passage to memorize and determine if this discipline would be helpful for you. Do not allow yourself to be intimidated by women who have more time or who are gifted differently.

Make your Bible study—whatever level you choose—top priority. Consider spacing your study throughout the week so that you can take time to ponder and meditate on what the Holy Spirit is teaching you. Do not make other appointments during the group Bible study. Ask God to enable you to attend faithfully. Come with an excitement to learn from others and a desire to share yourself and your journey. Give it your best, and God promises to join you on this adventure that can change your life.

Why Study Ecclesiastes?

Maybe you've tried to understand the book of Ecclesiastes in the past, but quit in verse two when you encountered the baffling stanza, "'Meaningless! Meaningless!' says the Teacher. 'Utterly meaningless! Everything is meaningless.'" If you endured further you may have found yourself discouraged, even slightly depressed, at questions like "What do people gain from all their labors at which they toil under the sun?"

You may have concluded: Life's hard enough. Why should I read a book written by a man who sounds like he's on the verge of suicide?

Would you be surprised if I told you that a thorough study of Ecclesiastes can actually lead to an optimistic outlook on life? It's true. In addition, this book will help you abandon habits, hang-ups, and foolish perspectives that keep you in bondage to everything that destroys the ultimate joy Jesus wants for you.

But to reap the treasures buried within its pages, you must study the twelve chapters of Ecclesiastes with the proper interpretive tools. You must understand why this book is included as a valuable voice in Scripture. You must approach its riches with a mind-set that will enable you to differentiate when the author speaks from a perverted worldly perspective—"under the sun"—and when he speaks from a godly perspective—"under the Son." Both appear side by side and are not always easy to decipher, but I'll draw from the finest scholars to help you differentiate as you progress.

The Bible contains different types of divine literature or genres, and we must not interpret them as if they were all the same.

There's a vast difference between the Hebrew poetry of the Psalms and the tightly argued epistles of Paul; between the grand, sweeping narrative of Genesis and Exodus, and the simple, poignant stories of the parables. There is allegory and love poetry, satire and apocalyptic, comedy and tragedy, and much more. The Holy Spirit used each of these forms to communicate His message. So if you want to grasp that message, you must read each kind according to its proper "rules." (Hendricks and Hendricks, *Living*, 38)

Ecclesiastes is included in the biblical genre called wisdom literature. As in the book of Proverbs, the writer takes on the role of a wise veteran ready to share his insights with someone who wants to learn how the world works and how to live well in it. It's full of nuggets of wisdom that reveal general principles about life and God. Wisdom literature doesn't contain promises from God that always apply to individual situations, but instead teaches readers how life works, what to pursue if they desire to make wise choices, and what to avoid when tempted to make foolish ones.

In Ecclesiastes, the author, Solomon, shares his journal, probably written over a period of years. He chronicles various experiences, sometimes expressed when he's walking close to God and sometimes when he's distant and even estranged from God. The different entries ping-pong between these two perspectives. When Solomon is walking close to God, his entries show us what godly living looks like, giving us a path to emulate. When he's not, we hear him espouse worldly, foolish, perverted ideas, giving us a path to avoid. Most of us can identify times when we've used similar foolish logic and suffered for it—live and learn. But now we have the opportunity to learn and then go out and live wisely, without the painful consequences that foolish decisions usually incur. At first reading, it's not always easy to identify Solomon's mood or perspective, but I'll help as you work your way through his journal. If you invest the time and energy, rich rewards await. Join me in an adventure through one of my favorite books of the Bible—Ecclesiastes.

 **Introduction to Studying Ecclesiastes** *(10:37 minutes).*

Under the Sun or Under the Son?

For centuries thoughtful people have asked, "What's the meaning of life? Who created all this? Why am I here? What's the best way to live out the years I've been given?" Varied answers abound, but I'm assuming that since you are holding a Bible study in your hands that you are interested in how the Bible answers these questions.

Would you like to read answers in the personal journal of the wisest man who ever lived? Then join me in a trek through Ecclesiastes. Usually journals contain secret thoughts and life lessons as the author walks through different experiences; these excerpts from Solomon's journal won't disappoint. They record his emotional ups and downs, inner struggles over the meaning of life, and verdicts of wisdom and futility.

His insights are exceptional because Solomon, unlike most people, enjoyed extravagant means to investigate unlimited options. What if you had the resources to test typical experiences to see if they answered the emptiness, disappointment, and injustice we all experience without God? What if you could experiment to see what truly satisfies and what's counterfeit? That's what Solomon did, and he recorded what he learned along the way.

Join Solomon on his personal research project to discover what matters and what doesn't. Then you won't have to experience the consequences and pain of your own poor choices and decisions. What a gift God is offering us!

You'll be challenged from time to time along the way. Solomon's journal writings are sometimes confusing, requiring us to decipher whether he is speaking from a foolish "under the sun" viewpoint or a wise perspective that keeps God in the picture. Discussing your ideas with others should help, and I'll provide notes and clues as we go.

Just as Solomon was willing to reflect and assess whether or not he was spending his life on what truly mattered, God is asking us to do the same. I promise that if you're willing, you'll emerge wiser and better equipped to live well in the demanding, complex, and sometimes even grim world where we find ourselves today. You'll discover sound biblical answers to those big questions: "What's the meaning of life? Who created all this? Why am I here? What's the best way to live out the years I've been given?" Knowing is the first step to living a life of peace, joy, and significance. Isn't that what we all want, and what the Lord wants for us? So get ready for an exciting adventure into the rich beauty and wisdom buried in Solomon's ancient yet timely journal entitled *Ecclesiastes*.

HISTORICAL BACKGROUND

Almost three thousand years ago, King Solomon wrote Ecclesiastes, a book of Hebrew poetry and wisdom literature. Solomon, the son of King David and his wife Bathsheba, served as the king of the united kingdom of Israel and Judah for forty years. He was known throughout history as the wisest man in the world. How did he become so wise? When he first became king, the Lord appeared to Solomon in a dream and said, "Ask for whatever you want me to give you" (1 Kings 3:5). Solomon asked for wisdom and knowledge to lead the people and to distinguish right from wrong (1 Kings 3:9). God granted his request. In addition, God gave Solomon great wealth, possessions, and honor (2 Chronicles 1:12). Kings all over the world sent emissaries to Solomon's court to learn from him (1 Kings 4:34).

Solomon's name means "peace" and "prosperity." During his reign, Israel experienced national peace and enormous affluence. However, the common people were also burdened with heavy taxation and many were forced to leave their jobs and families to construct Solomon's massive building projects (1 Kings 11:28; 12:4). Renowned for seven hundred wives and three hundred concubines, Solomon allowed himself and his people to be corrupted by pagan religious practices introduced as the result of his intermarriage with foreign women to cement alliances with other nations (1 Kings 11:1–6). The wisest man in the world did not always follow the wisdom of the Lord.

 Read Ecclesiastes 1:1–11.

WHY BOTHER? A SKEWED VIEW WITHOUT GOD

In the first two verses, Solomon identifies himself as the author and titles his journal with a blaring headline: *Meaningless! Meaningless! Utterly meaningless! Everything is meaningless.*

Please don't snap this study guide shut and walk away, assuming it's a downer leading to depression and hopelessness. Two additional words will become clear as you journey through Solomon's entries: Without God. *Meaningless, Meaningless! Utterly meaningless! Without God everything is meaningless.* But do you really believe it, or, like most people, are you still

---

DIGGING DEEPER

Read the account of the Queen of Sheba's visit to Solomon in 1 Kings 10:1–13. Why did she visit him? What did she learn that overwhelmed her? Who did she praise for putting Solomon on the throne and specifically why? What does her trip assessment tell you about Solomon's early reign?

The vision of the Preacher alternates between a narrow perspective and a broad perspective. In the narrow perspective, he walks by sight, seeing only what happens "under the sun." When he sees existence from this narrow perspective, he is full of questions. When he sees the broad perspective, and walks by faith, he finds a partial answer. He glimpses God and eternity and realizes that here lies the meaning of life. Because Jesus has not yet been revealed, his answer is only partial. We must be constantly aware of which of these two perspectives the Preacher is viewing or we won't understand the passage and may make the error of applying the short-sighted conclusions of the narrow perspective to our lives.
—Dee Brestin
(*Ecclesiastes*, 11)

attempting to satisfy your yearnings in all the wrong places? Stick with Solomon to squelch those desires for good.

1. The Hebrew word often translated as "meaningless" or "vanity" is *hebel*. Other translations would be "like a vapor," "passing away swiftly," "breath," or "mist." Read verse 2 aloud, substituting one of these words or phrases for meaningless or vanity. How does this change your understanding of what Solomon might be attempting to communicate?

2. Solomon's father, David, also used the word *hebel* in Psalm 39:5 and Psalm 103:13–17. Compare these passages with James 4:14. What truth do you learn? Why do you think Solomon, David, and James are all pleading with us to remember this truth?

DIGGING DEEPER

Read 1 Kings 3:5–14. What did God ask Solomon? What did God give Solomon in addition to his request? How did God ask Solomon to put his wisdom into action and what was the promised result?

Vanity is used at least three ways in the book:
1. *fleeting*—vapor-like or transitory nature of life
2. *futile*—cursed condition of earth and its effect on man
3. *incomprehensible or unknowable*—life's unanswerable questions; the mysteries of God's purposes
—adapted from John MacArthur (*MacArthur Bible Handbook*, 172)

3. Throughout his life, Solomon attempted to find fulfillment, satisfaction, and meaning apart from God in a variety of experiences, projects, and accomplishments. Many are listed below. Not all are entirely worthless but most promise what, ultimately, they cannot deliver. As you examine the list, ask the Holy Spirit to red-flag ones that excite or woo you with promises of fulfillment, satisfaction, and meaning apart from God. Be honest. If you are bold enough, mark them.

making people laugh	the newest technology
significant career	birthing and raising children
comfort	helping people
pets/animals	earning credentials
titles	leading others
pleasure	great sex
alcohol	night life in clubs and bars
entertainment	beautiful shoes
ego-building projects	a large, beautiful home
decorating/redecorating	art collections (or other collecting)
travel/fun trips	weight loss goals
exercise/physical fitness	flirting/romantic teasing
forbidden relationships	social media
health	cosmetics/makeovers
fashion/dressing well	athletic ability/competitions
music	being young
receiving lots of attention	wealth/security
leaving a legacy	being smart
being respected	being loved
drugs/prescription medications	adventure
being the boss	being remembered
stress-free life	outdoor sports
having great friends	a strong man who adores me
being skilled at ____________	nature, beauty, and a green thumb
being free from ____________	fine cuisine
Netflix marathons	an apology from ____________
other ____________	other ____________

For pondering: Do you value anything on the above list more than you value your relationship with God? If so, any insight into why?

4. We can know what someone values by looking at their calendar to see how they spend their time and by looking at their bank account to see how they spend their money. Take an honest look at your calendar and bank account. What does this reveal about you and what you value? What changes would you like to see over the course of our study in Ecclesiastes?

5. Consider a time when you expected to find meaning, fulfillment, or satisfaction in an experience, project, or accomplishment, but were disappointed. What happened? Why were you disappointed? What did you learn?

You may judge a man by what he groans after.
—Charles Spurgeon
(*Evening by Evening*, 341)

6. Solomon asks a disturbing question in verse 3. Paraphrase the question in your own words. Can you remember a specific time when you asked the same question? What prompted the question?

7. How would you answer Solomon's question in verse 3? Does your daily work seem meaningless or does it have purpose and significance? Explain.

Note that Solomon uses the phrase "under the sun" in verse 3. Whenever you see this phrase, realize that he is talking about life without God in the picture. Throughout Ecclesiastes, he contrasts his perspectives when he leaves God out with wise nuggets of truth that include God. As a result, as Solomon writes, we'll observe dramatic changes in his heart attitude, direction, and conclusions.

But haven't you and I experienced the same kinds of shifts in our own thinking from time to time? We get caught up in our everyday concerns and situations, and suddenly we find ourselves thinking like we did before we came into a relationship with Jesus. Before we may have known God was "God" but not that he was *our* heavenly Father, *our* Savior, *our* Redeemer, the Lover of *our* souls. Some of us practiced a religion with rules, but God seemed distant and we felt alone. And if we're honest with ourselves, sometimes we go back there. Back to the confusion, clouded reasoning, and foolish inclinations that take hold . . . until we look up and realize that we have forgotten how much God loves us and have neglected to include him in our thinking.

If we are wise, we once again throw ourselves on the mercy of our great God. He forgives, comforts, and graciously guides us into right thinking and actions. Solomon experienced similar vacillations in his spiritual life. As we journey through his journal we'll see these patterns and ultimately what he learned. Solomon lived and learned the hard way, the painful way. But God preserved Ecclesiastes so that we could learn and then go out and live with wisdom, peace, and hope.

ROUND AND ROUND, WHAT'S THE POINT?

8. As Solomon surveys life "under the sun" he comes to the conclusion that nature is cyclical. List the examples he provides in the following verses:

verse 4   verse 5

verse 6   verse 7

9. How does his awareness of unending cycles affect his mood (1:8)? Why do you think these kinds of insights tend to discourage or depress us?

10. Reread verses 9–10. In the preceding section, Solomon illustrates life's circular pattern using nature. Now he takes his illustrations from history where mankind is the main participant. What do you learn about life from these verses?

SO, WHAT'S NEW?

11. In what sense is "there is nothing new under the sun" true? In what sense might some people disagree?

12. What's Solomon's point in verse 11? How far back do you remember your ancestors? How far into the future do you think people will remember you?

13. How do you feel as you ponder the implications of verse 11? How might this reality affect you if you yearn to make a name for yourself or if you easily get caught up in people-pleasing?

14. Although your ancestors or future relatives won't remember you, who will (Isaiah 43:1–2, 5–7; Revelation 2:17)? What do these truths reveal about the reasons God created you? About how much God loves you?

Just to put into perspective the brevity of our lives: Throughout time, somewhere between forty-five billion and one hundred twenty-five billion people have lived on this earth. That's 125,000,000,000. In about fifty years (give or take a couple of decades), no one will remember you. Everyone you know will be dead. Certainly no one will care what job you had, what car you drove, what school you attended, or what clothes you wore. This can be terrifying or reassuring, or maybe a mix of both.
—Francis Chan
(*Crazy Love*, 45–46)

I attend a rigorous water aerobics class for seniors done to the music of our generation. Our instructor, a senior herself, likes to tease the teen lifeguard who watches over us by asking him if he recognizes the vocalists—famous people, to seniors anyway, like Frank Sinatra and Tina Turner. Every time he responds with a blank look and a bit of an embarrassed smirk, Solomon's words echo in my mind, "No one remembers the former generations, and even those yet to come will not be remembered by those who follow them" (Ecclesiastes 1:11). So why do so many people yearn to make a name for themselves and let other people have such power over them? God alone remembers our names. —Sue

15. In his first journal entry (1:3–11), Solomon seems to be struggling with a skewed perspective, possibly even depression. Have you ever struggled with such a deep sadness that it colored your heart attitude toward everything in your life? Do you sometimes still feel that way? (If so, please seek the help of a trusted counselor and medical professional.) If you have found your way out of the darkness, what helped?

We live in a fallen world—and so did Solomon, a king with unlimited resources and human power. In his journal entries, we observe him coming to terms with reality—bad things happen to everyone for a variety of reasons. As we finish up our first lesson, let's consider some of the explanations, as well as a reason to look up and find hope in God's ultimate plan for humanity.

The Bible reveals how God created the earth, a beautiful place he originally designed for us to live. We find these truths in the first two chapters of Genesis. But in chapter three we learn that our ancestors decided to rebel against God, thus ushering sin into the world. With sin came destruction, disintegration, and physical death. But because of God's strong love for us, the masterpiece of his creation and the apple of his eye, he immediately implemented his plan to redeem and restore the fallen world.

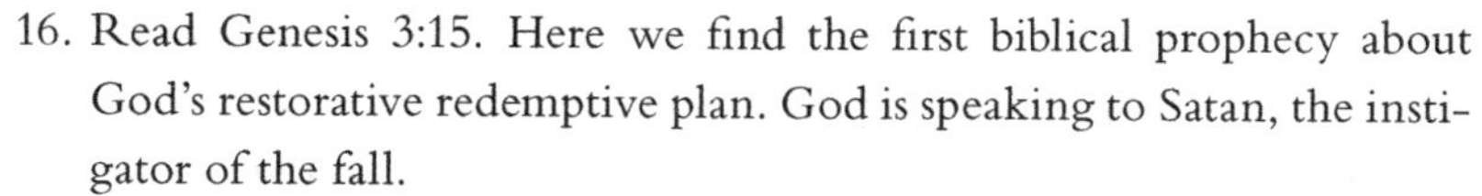

16. Read Genesis 3:15. Here we find the first biblical prophecy about God's restorative redemptive plan. God is speaking to Satan, the instigator of the fall.

What is enmity?

What do you think God might mean when he says that he will put enmity between Satan and the woman, and between Satan's offspring and her offspring? (See Matthew 1:20–21; 4:8–10.)

Who might God be referring to where it says that "he" will crush your head? Who crushed Satan's head? (See 1 John 3:8; Romans 16:20; Luke 4:31–37.)

How did Satan strike his heel? (See Luke 18:31–33.) How is striking the heel different from crushing the head?

The Bible is jam-packed with prophecies that reveal God's ultimate plan to redeem and restore the world. Read Revelation 21:1–4 and 22:1–5 for a peek into God's new creation.

Yet right now we still must make our way in a fallen world. When Solomon forgot God's promises and left God out of the picture, he concluded, "Meaningless! Meaningless! Everything is meaningless." And if we

DIGGING DEEPER

For more insight into the creation and fall, work through the verses and questions below.

- Read the first chapter of Genesis. Was there frustration in the world ("meaninglessness") when God originally created it?
- What did God ask of Adam and Eve in Genesis 2:15–17?
- What happened (Genesis 3:6)?
- Finally, read Genesis 3:14–19. List everything that was affected by Adam and Eve's decision to listen to the serpent and disobey God.
- As a result, why do we experience frustration in the world now?

leave God out of the picture, we too can come to similar conclusions. But they are flawed. Spend this season of study asking God to show you areas of your life where you are saddled with "under the sun" perspectives. Your future and your legacy are at stake and a whole-hearted love relationship with God will make all the difference. Be encouraged.

When Having It All Isn't Enough

LESSON 2

Most of us can easily think of a celebrity or possibly even someone we know who has suffered the soul wrenching effects of depression. Someone who seemed to have it all, until the empty God-shaped vacuum within swallowed them up like a black hole. It's heartbreaking to watch, and agonizing to be the one who is suffering. I know. I've been in that dark place.

Depression is a beast that takes you places you never thought you could go and do things you never thought you would do. But in the grips of depression, you hurt so bad and your thinking is so skewed that you commit outrageous acts, often against yourself. You become your own worst enemy.

In my twenties, before I found the Lord and even early in my Christian journey, I battled depression. I was raised in a pagan home by a mother who didn't love me, which saddled me with wrong thinking and deep pain. I bought into the lie that we evolved out of slime and are only here for a short time, so grab what you can. I desperately wanted to be loved and for my life to make a difference, but I was clueless and foolish. I had not done business with the demons in my life, and if Jesus hadn't rescued me, I probably would have ended up dead.

But thank you, God, my neighbor two doors down cared enough to befriend me and to invite me to a women's Bible study. At the time, I was a mess. David and I were married with two beautiful baby daughters, but I had no idea how to be the wife he needed or how to parent well. My dear father had just lost his five year battle with cancer. And I was cycling between days of depression and days where I could function. I loved my husband and those two baby girls more than life itself, but I couldn't figure life out. Thus, many weekends I spent glued to a living room chair, immobilized, as I sunk deeper and deeper into despair. This dark night of the soul, the place where I came to the end of myself, was exactly what prepared me for the beauty of God, his Word, and the women he used to pull me out of that canyon of terror.

The community of women God placed me in encircled me with care. Interestingly, for the next six years, my children were never sick on Bible study day. Little by little, the depression lifted as I learned that although my mother did not love me, God loved me, and God became my perfect parent. As I studied the Scriptures I learned wisdom, skill in everyday living, and I became a voracious reader of the Bible and books by godly Christian authors. They all mentored me. Fifteen years later I was teaching women the Bible and attending seminary to become a better Bible teacher.

Women in that Bible study saw potential in me that I never saw in myself, and they invested in me. I began to invest in others and found a healthy church where I could serve. Over the years that black hole of emptiness filled and healed as I grew stronger in the Lord. Depression has not plagued me for over thirty years. Praise God! I don't know if I'll ever battle it again. I hope that the well of inner strength will be enough should life implode again. I'm trusting in God's grace.

Many people that look like they have it all are miserable inside. In college I took a philosophy course and learned that many of the "great" secular thinkers throughout history committed suicide. Many of us look at comedians, film stars, sports giants, and billionaires as people who have it all, but without God in the picture, people ultimately come to the same conclusion as Solomon: *Meaningless! Meaningless! Life without God is meaningless.*

What are the lessons for us? Are you holding out on God, still secretly believing you can find significance and meaning in life apart from God? Is your heart divided? God is not asking you to live a secluded life in a monastery somewhere. He desires that you engage in the world as his daughter, taking his hand every step of the way. Solomon calls out from the past, "I tried it all and nothing satisfies without God. Learn from me and save yourself the agony."

Also, many of us back off sharing our faith with people who seem to have it all. We think they don't know they need God. They won't listen. But we never know what's going on in someone's heart or behind closed doors. Live so the world sees Jesus honored. Be unashamed to tell others what he's doing in your life. With gentleness and respect (1 Peter 3:15), show and tell others about the only One who can fill that empty God-shaped vacuum within all of us. He's the only one who is enough.

 ## Read Ecclesiastes 1:12–18.

INTELLECTUAL PURSUITS WITHOUT GOD

1. Now Solomon records the beginning of his search for meaning in life. Where does he look first (1:13)?

2. Solomon says he devoted himself "to study and to explore by wisdom all that is done under the heavens." To understand what he means, we must differentiate between the two kinds of wisdom in Scripture, and then determine which kind Solomon is referring to. Start by reading James 3:13–18.

What are the two kinds of wisdom?

List characteristics and the end results of each.

Which kind do you think Solomon was referring to in 1:12–18?

3. Why do you think Solomon calls this kind of wisdom "a heavy burden" in verse 13? Have you ever pursued academics without God in the picture, or academics whose goal was to discredit God? If so, what did you learn?

4. What does the author conclude about this kind of wisdom in 1:18 and 12:12?

5. Verse 14 is one of the theme verses in the book. Consider characteristics of the wind. What do you think it means to "chase after the wind"? How much of your life this week have you spent "chasing after the wind"?

6. Job, an Old Testament nomad who lived during the time of Abraham, knew that godly wisdom could not be found through intellectual pursuits without God. Read Job 28:12–28 to learn where to find godly wisdom.

If you want godly wisdom, what is your best resource (Job 28:23; Hebrews 4:12)?

How can you make this resource a greater priority in your life?

Reread Job 28:28 aloud. What is the first step toward acquiring godly wisdom?

What is "the fear of the Lord"?

Why do you think wisdom also includes putting what we know into action?

7. If you attain godly wisdom, how do you think your daily life might change?

 Read Ecclesiastes 2:1–11.

PURSUING PLEASURE, POPULARITY, POSSESSIONS, AND PROJECTS WITHOUT GOD

In 2:1, Solomon writes, "Come now, I will test you with pleasure to find out what is good." Remember that he's talking about experimenting with pleasure without considering God or God's instructions concerning life's pleasures.

8. What are a couple of things Solomon experimented with (2:2)?

9. In verse 2, the author says, "Laughter is madness." Like wisdom, the Bible reveals two kinds of humor and laughter. Compare them in Proverbs 26:18–19 and 17:22. How are they different? What kind of laughter do you think he is talking about in verse 2?

10. How do contemporary comedians demonstrate the kind of mad laughter Solomon talks about in verse 2? Do you know anyone who uses humor to protect themselves or tear down others? (No names, please.) Why is this kind of laughter so destructive and meaningless?

11. What do you find most pleasurable in life? Have you included God in these pleasures? What might be some ways to do that?

12. Where else did Solomon look for meaning in life (2:4–6)? Picture these endeavors in your mind. Would you enjoy losing yourself in a project like this? Why or why not?

13. Are these kinds of projects wrong in themselves? Did Solomon find any fulfillment in his accomplishments (2:10)? What is his ultimate conclusion (2:11)?

14. Why do you think Solomon is sharing these entries in his journal with us? What difference might it make in our future lives if we spent some time honestly assessing ways we might be like Solomon?

15. Where else did he look for meaning (2:7–8)? What are some specific modern-day equivalents?

His [God's] feelings exist in relation to us. His jealous rage and tenderness burn against Christians guilty of idolatry, guilty of holding material things in higher regard than God. We do well to tremble lest we forget who we are, from whence we came and to whom we belong. For our God is a God of fire.
—John White
(*Golden Cow*, 25)

16. How does our culture encourage us to follow Solomon's example in verses 7 and 8?

17. On a scale of 1 to 10, how vulnerable are you to our culture's message that stuff ensures happiness? Name ways to overcome unhealthy temptations related to materialism.

18. The Bible speaks often about our relationship to the material world. In your own words, summarize the wise approach of Proverbs 30:7–9 as we relate to money and the material world.

19. Solomon looked for meaning in life in another way in verse 9. What is it?

20. Can you discern why obtaining this kind of status is attractive to so many people today? If you struggle with this too, can you discern why? If you are comfortable doing so, please share. If you have overcome this temptation, share what might help others still struggling.

21. In this journal entry, Solomon introduces us to his primary attempts to find meaning in life apart from God: intellectual pursuits, pleasures, projects, possessions, and popularity. He'll elaborate on each in later journal entries. As you consider them all, which still exerts power over you, drawing you away from a healthy, intimate relationship with God? Ask the Holy Spirit to open your eyes to these temptations so that you can pursue a life full of lasting meaning and fulfillment, bringing glory to God and joy to you and others around you.

Investing in Future Generations | LESSON 3

What long-term good will result from your years on earth? Generations before us have had profound effects on us, whether we remember their names or not. Over five hundred times the Bible exhorts us to pass on our faith to upcoming generations. The church is always only one generation away from extinction in any given society, although God promises that his church will always thrive somewhere. God gives us different ways to influence those who come behind us.

We all have opportunities to influence spiritual children in our communities through mentoring, discipling, coaching, and friendship with other generations. Some of us raise biological children, and some of them bring tremendous joy to their families and society, while others bring disappointment. Disappointing behaviors are not always the result of healthy or unhealthy parenting, although good parenting certainly gives children advantages. But ultimately, children exercise free will in whether or not they will love God and how they will spend their lives.

In this lesson, we observe Solomon asking himself what long-term good will result from his years on earth. He comes to several conclusions, some wise and others skewed. It's easy to see why, when we consider Solomon's choices and the lineage he left behind. First Kings 11:3 tells us that Solomon had seven hundred wives and three hundred concubines. He married many foreign women to secure political alliances and these women brought their pagan religions and temples to Israel with them. Imagine the controversy at the breakfast table!

We can reasonably speculate that he fathered hundreds of children. Of these, his son Rehoboam succeeded him, but Rehoboam was so disliked by the people that the united kingdom split. Ultimately Rehoboam only ruled over the southern tribe of Judah, and Jeroboam, one of Solomon's early officials who later rebelled, ruled over the northern kingdom, Israel.

Obviously, Solomon's home life was a mess, resulting in serious consequences for his family and God's people. His concerns about his legacy were well founded. What about yours? As you dig into this lesson's journal entries, consider your own legacy and how to pass on your faith to those who follow you. And learn from Solomon's foolish choices.

OPTIONAL

Memorize Deuteronomy 6:6–7
These commandments that I give you today are to be on your hearts. Impress them on your children. Talk about them when you sit at home and when you walk along the road, when you lie down and when you get up.

Read Ecclesiastes 2:12–23.

THE ADVANTAGES OF WISDOM

Journals often reflect the emotional ups and downs of their authors. Some people verbally process their reactions to their experiences and others process by writing down what they feel. For Solomon, this processing led to parts of his journal reflecting foolish ideas and other parts reflecting wisdom. We observe the first example of wise conclusions in 2:12–14.

1. Earlier in his journal, Solomon insinuates that wisdom is worthless (1:2, 12–18). But now he comes to a different, wiser conclusion. What does he say in 2:12–14?

2. However, something upsets him, causing him to revert to his bleak outlook. What is "one fate" which befalls both the wise and the foolish (2:14)? Is his realization true or false? How do you feel about this?

3. Solomon asks himself a question in 2:15 and goes on to answer it in verse 16. What does he conclude? How would you respond if Solomon asked you the same question?

Old Testament saints did not have the full understanding of eternal life that the New Testament provides. They did not know that God would send his Son, Jesus, to die for our sins, and change the way we view death. Even so, the Old Testament provides clear truth that eternal life was available for God's beloved, truth that Solomon should have known if he spent time in God's Word.

4. Read the following passages and identify what each of these Old Testament authors believed about eternal life.

Job 19:25–26

Psalm 16:7–11 (written by Solomon's father, David)

Proverbs 12:28 (This was written by Solomon himself, earlier in life. Why might Solomon have forgotten this truth?)

Because we retain our flesh, or sin nature, even after we become a new creation in Christ, we struggle to overcome sinful desires and distorted perspectives, even when we know better. Read Romans 7:14–25. How does Paul reflect what is probably happening within Solomon as he writes Ecclesiastes? What benefits do we enjoy as new-covenant Christians that were not available to Solomon (Galatians 5:13–18)?

LEAVING A LEGACY

5. Solomon despaired as he faced death. Do you find it difficult to think or talk about death and dying? If so, why? If you belong to Christ, what will happen to you when your life on earth is over (see 2 Corinthians 5:1–8)?

6. What especially irritated Solomon about dying (2:18–21)? What do his fears reveal about his relationships with his hundreds of children?

Whether you raise little ones in your home or nurture spiritual children in your faith community, we are all called to help grow up the generations behind us by passing on our faith. If we do, we probably won't feel as grieved as Solomon when we contemplate our own physical death. Consider the passages in the following questions to help you become productive mentors with successive generations.

7. As the Israelites were entering the promised land, God instructed them as a faith community to mentor future generations. Read Deuteronomy 6:4–9 and Psalm 78:4. What are some of the most effective ways to leave a legacy through mentoring according to Deuteronomy 6:7?

DIGGING DEEPER

Any thoughts on the meanings of Deuteronomy 6:8–9? Feel free to use commentaries for clues. What might this look like today?

On one of Paul's missionary journeys he mentored a young man named Titus. Together they planted a number of churches on the Greek island of Crete. When Paul left to plant other churches, Titus remained to oversee the Cretan churches. Paul wrote a letter back to Titus to help him lead these new faith communities well. We glean valuable insight to help us create healthy mentoring ministries today from Paul's letter to Titus.

 **Read Titus 2:1–5.**

8. What does Paul say should be their ministries' first priority (2:1)? What are different ways faith communities can accomplish this with various groups?

After Paul instructs Titus regarding the men in the churches, he relays important principles required for the women to grow up in their faith.

9. Paul tells Titus to identify two groups of women. Who are they (2:3–4)?

10. Few first-century women in Crete had the benefit of a formal education, requiring Titus to invest in this first generation of spiritually maturing women. What qualities did he need to look for as well as attempt to develop in them (2:3)?

The Greek word for "teach" in verse 3 is the same word used of Jesus or a rabbi when they formally taught students. The Greek word for "urge," more accurately translated as "train," in verse 4 is a completely different word that describes a mentor or coach who walks alongside an apprentice to model wise, practical life skills. The two main tracks a ministry to women should run on are the teaching of Scripture and the training of life skills. If a ministry to women highlights these two core priorities, teaching and training, it has the essence of what it takes to help women grow strong in the faith.   —Sue

Fruitful mentoring includes the ingredients of transparency, authenticity, developing friendship, and truth, as well as the investment of time, prayer, and most of all agape love. Not only because of the Titus 2 biblical mandate but also because I have known the incredible value of older women investing in younger women, I have made it a lifelong priority to be intentionally involved in mentoring women.
— Cynthia Hester, seminary intern

DIGGING DEEPER

What do you learn about the mentoring relationship between Jesus's mother, Mary, and her older relative Elizabeth from Luke 1:39–56?

11. Once these women were sufficiently prepared to invest in the next generation, what two kinds of ministries were they told to focus on (2:3–4)?

12. Have you ever enjoyed a quality mentoring relationship, as either a mentor or a mentee? If so, describe the relationship and why it worked for you.

13. What kind of a legacy would you like to leave behind? What are some ways to make that legacy a reality?

14. Solomon asks and answers another question in Ecclesiastes 2:22–23. Describe his attitude about work. Discuss the interchange.

15. Have you ever asked yourself what you get "for all the toil"? What are your frustrations or joys about your work?

16. What helpful strategies have you found to cope with our 24/7 fast-paced, technology-driven work world?

God created his daughters to be kingdom builders—to pay attention to what is happening around us, to take action and contribute. . . . There's no age requirement for kingdom building and no expiration date when we retire. . . . We may retire from our jobs. The nest may empty. We may lose our health. But God's image bearers remain on active duty. I've known young girls who were steadfastly kingdom minded and elderly women in nursing homes who were diligently going about God's business when the clock ran out. God never retires his image bearers.
—Carolyn Custis James
(*Half the Church*, 76–78)

Because of all this technology, our world has changed so drastically over the last fifty years that the biblical character Abraham of 2000 B.C. would probably have more in common with Abraham Lincoln of the early 1800s than Lincoln would have with us in the twenty-first century. . . . When we fail to recognize the impact of such technological change, we run the risk of allowing our tools to dictate our methods. Technology should not dictate our values or our methods. Rather, we must use technology *out of* our convictions and values.
—John Dyer (*From the Garden to the City*, 21, 25)

17. If you can, describe a personal experience that caused you to reevaluate putting a lot of time and energy into something transitory.

 Read Ecclesiastes 2:24–26.

In these verses, Solomon takes stock of all he has learned from his search for meaning thus far and records another wise excerpt to help us navigate the complexities of our lives.

STOP AND SMELL THE ROSES

18. What is the best way for us to live (2:24–25)? This is a different philosophy from the hedonist's motto: "Eat, drink, and be merry, for tomorrow we die." How do you think it is different?

19. Who makes a satisfying life possible?

20. Are you truly able to enjoy the simple pleasures of life? Do you stop and take time to smell the roses? What would need to change in your life for you to savor your relationships, work, and meals more?

21. What are some of the other gifts that God bestows upon those who please him (2:26)? Do you possess these gifts from God?

22. What kinds of frustrations can those who ignore God expect (2:26)?

To ponder: Would you characterize yourself right now more as the person who pleases God or more as the person who ignores God? What's your satisfaction level with your life right now? Stick with us in our jaunt through Solomon's journal because God loves you and wants your satisfaction level to go sky high and God will show you how in the weeks ahead.

Your Life—Beautiful or Burdensome?

LESSON 4

A portion of the journal entry we'll study now became the popular hit song "Turn! Turn! Turn!" performed by the Byrds in 1962. Many people know the words but few truly understand their meanings—that's our current task. In seven verses, Solomon lists twenty-eight events and activities, fourteen pairs of polar opposites. They symbolize the whole gamut of our life's experiences. But his point is not easy to discern. Our goal is to see if we can figure out what he's trying to communicate, and when we get it, we'll glean a significant truth to help us lay aside our burdens and exchange them for the beautiful abundant life God offers.

As we begin, consider this prophecy about Jesus the Messiah from Isaiah 61:1–3:

> The Spirit of the Sovereign LORD is on me, because the LORD has anointed me to proclaim good news to the poor. He has sent me to bind up the brokenhearted, to proclaim freedom for the captives and release from darkness for the prisoners, to proclaim the year of the LORD's favor and the day of vengeance of our God, to comfort all who mourn, and provide for those who grieve in Zion—to bestow on them a crown of beauty instead of ashes, the oil of joy instead of mourning, and a garment of praise instead of a spirit of despair.

Read Ecclesiastes 3:1–11.

1. Meditate on verse 1. What do you think Solomon is saying? Share a circumstance that you have faced when recalling this verse might have helped you reframe the situation.

2. Look over the contrasts in verses 2–8. Make a list of events or activities that you believe are beautiful. Make a list of the events or activities that you consider burdensome.

3. Solomon asks a question in verse 9 and answers the questions in verse 10. What word does Solomon use to describe our lives in verse 10? What is his perspective "under the sun"?

4. Now Solomon changes his tune. In the first sentence of verse 11, how does Solomon describe what God can do in our lives?

5. Look back over the list of events and activities you marked in question 2. Consider again the ones you marked as burdensome. Give some examples of ways God might make these situations beautiful.

6. Can you remember a time when God redeemed a difficult, even pain-ful, event in your life so that now you can call it "beautiful"? If you are comfortable, tell your group about it, what God did, and how you feel about it now.

A CLOSER LOOK AT THE CONTRASTS

Some of these events and activities seem to concern physical activities; for example, for a farmer, a time to plant and a time to uproot. But the same pair could also represent something different to someone else, possibly a time when we put down roots in a community and then a time we deter-mine we need to move. Others seem to focus on emotional seasons: for example, a time to weep and a time to laugh, or a time to embrace and a time to refrain from embracing. Each pair represents a variety of differ-ent situations we will likely experience in our lifetime, some pleasurable, others painful, some because we live in a fallen world, others because we make wise or poor choices, but all under the ultimate sovereign hand of a loving God.

As a result, these events and activities take on different meanings depending on whether we view them through pagan eyes or through the eyes of someone who loves God and includes God in each event and activity.

7. Solomon begins the list of life's events and activities with a contrast that encompasses all the others—*a time to be born and a time to die.* How much control do you have over these two events in your life? How do you feel about that reality?

8. Pick out several of the pairs that jump out at you because they seem to describe something you've personally experienced. What happened? Did you view those experiences through the lens of faith, including God in the picture? If so, how did that affect your attitude, assumptions, and actions? If not, how did that affect your attitude, assumptions, and actions?

9. Keeping God in the picture, under what circumstances might it be appropriate to:

uproot

kill

weep

refrain from embracing

give up

throw away

hate

make war

10. Most of us will probably experience many of these "times" in our lives. How do you feel about dealing with the more difficult experiences such as: *a time to uproot, to mourn, to weep, to give up, or to tear down?* Do you tend to always view these experiences as burdens (2:23)?

11. How might keeping God in the picture change your perspective, making these experiences less difficult to bear, possibly even beautiful (3:11)?

12. The second pair in verse 7 teaches us that there is a time to be silent and a time to speak. What problems have you encountered when you spoke at the wrong time instead of remaining silent?

Describe some situations when you would have been wiser to speak up.

How might keeping God in the picture make us wiser as we communicate with others?

You can't carry yourself through the storms; it's too much for you. When will we come to the realization that the blizzards in our lives are allowed by God? Those threatening storms are designed to slow us down, to make us climb up into His arms, to force us to depend on Him.
—Charles Swindoll (*Three Steps Forward*, 46)

13. Solomon observes another important truth in 3:11. What do you think it means that we have "eternity" in our hearts? How does this distinguish us from animals?

DIGGING DEEPER

Read Isaiah 40:10–31. What attributes of God are evident? What truths emerge from this glorious divine literature about the nature of the God who created all things and rules with wisdom, power, and perfection? How does this marvelous poetry relate to the passage we are studying?

14. Compare the last part of 3:11 with the last part of 11:5. Now read Isaiah 55:8. What is the main point of these verses?

15. Most of us have felt that God's plans, ways, and times were sometimes different from ours. Give an example if you can. How do you tend to think and act if you find yourself disagreeing with God?

16. In his young adult years, the apostle Paul, formerly Saul in the New Testament, found himself directly opposed to God's plans for his life. Read Acts 26:9–11 where he describes his former life. But then Jesus appeared to him on the road to Damascus and called him to a new life, loving and serving Christ. Read Acts 26:12–18. What did Jesus say to him (v. 14)?

17. A goad is a long, sharp instrument used in biblical times to direct and keep oxen in line as they carried large loads. What do you think Jesus meant when he told Paul, "It is hard for you to kick against the goads"?

Farmers used long poles called goads to guide massive oxen along canals and roadways, keeping them from injuring themselves and making them useful to their masters. Goads in Scripture are words which nudge us into thinking biblically. Sometimes they are unpleasant, difficult to hear and grasp, but ultimately they are for our own good and God uses them to grow us into mature all-in Christ followers. —Sue

18. As Solomon concludes his journal, he says, "The words of the wise are like goads . . ." (12:11). What do you think he means? Why do you think Solomon refers to parts of his journal as "goads"?

By thoroughly disgusting us with the world, and by making us realize its absolute vanity, God means to draw us to himself. Only in this way can Jahveh, the true and absolute Being, become to us what he really is. Through much tribulation must our hold on earthly things be loosened and ourselves enter into the kingdom of God.
—Ernst Hengstenberg (*Commentary on Ecclesiastes*, 126)

19. How might what you are learning from Solomon's journal help you not to "kick against the goads"?

Read Ecclesiastes 3:12–15, 22.

THE "BE HAPPY AND DO GOOD" REFRAIN

Five times in Ecclesiastes, Solomon repeats the refrain, "Be happy and do good," each time with a little different twist and nuance. As you encounter these refrains, attempt to discern the added insight.

20. In light of verse 11, what does Solomon conclude about life in verses 12–15, and 22? Who alone makes this possible? What changes would you need to make to apply these verses?

21. Have you heard people insinuate that truly committed Christians are the kind of people who give up everything, go to Africa, and constantly suffer for God? Although these are admirable traits and required of some Christians, how does Solomon's conclusion conflict with that assumption (vv. 12–13)? How might Solomon's conclusion change some people's view of God's heart?

22. Why does God do what he does (3:14)? What do you think this means? What does this have to do with keeping God in the picture as you live out the events and activities in your life?

"IT'S NOT FAIR"

23. From what perspective does Solomon view the world (v. 16)? How do you know? Have you experienced this too?

24. How do you feel when you experience or observe injustice? When do you think people should experience consequences for what they do?

25. What is God's perspective and instruction concerning injustice (see Romans 12:17–19)? How does God's timing often compare with ours?

26. What does Solomon finally conclude (3:17; 8:11–13)? How might this view of justice help you as you consider how to redeem your burdens, turning them into something beautiful?

 Read Ecclesiastes 3:18–22.

Again, Solomon slips back into his depressed, perverted perspective "under the sun." (We might call this the "Eeyore Syndrome.")

27. How does he view humans in verse 18? In what ways are people and animals alike (3:19–20)?

28. How are people and animals different according to Genesis 1:27? Are people simply a higher form of animal—a product of time and chance as Darwin proposes in his theory of evolution? In what other ways are we different from animals?

I spent my growing up years, including college, believing that I'd find meaning and fulfillment through accomplishments and acclaim, which led to frustrating and impossible perfectionism and people-pleasing. But God was merciful. He allowed me to experience both accomplishments and acclaim in college, and both left me empty and depressed. As someone said back then, I was climbing the ladder to success and found I had placed it against the wrong building. I learned early that these earthly "treasures" are indeed "vanity" and "a chasing after the wind."

How kind of God to preserve Solomon's ancient journal for us so none of us has to learn these lessons the hard way—except those of us so hardheaded that we need to experience these painful lessons on our own. Don't go there—it's agonizing. Diligently dig into his journal; let God pry your grip off the counterfeit so you are free to take the hand of a real loving Father where you'll find deep peace, joy, and meaning.   —Sue

29. Have you learned anything new from Ecclesiastes chapter 3 about the character of God, how he relates to humanity, or how God wants you to live your life? If so, please share it with the group. How will you live differently this week in light of these new revelations?

Wise Up! | LESSON 5

Wise Up! | LESSON 5

What can we learn from Solomon as we attempt to exchange our burdens for a beautiful life? We must pursue wisdom—skill in living—as our first priority. We'll need to make wise choices in a culture where foolish choices are sometimes more popular. We'll need to perform for an audience of One, instead of worrying so much about what people think. We'll need to develop a kind, unselfish heart attitude to represent Christ well with our loved ones, as we work, and as we go about our daily routines. In short, we desperately need God's wisdom and discernment, and he wants to give it to us. But God won't play games with us. He won't give us wisdom unless he knows that we are serious about living out what we learn. But if we are, he promises to empower us:

> If any of you lacks wisdom, you should ask God, who gives generously to all without finding fault, and it will be given to you. But when you ask, you must believe and not doubt, because the one who doubts is like a wave of the sea, blown and tossed by the wind. (James 1:5–6)

In this lesson's journal entries, Solomon covers various topics to help us become more skilled at everyday living—topics like politics and money, sacred worship, the folly of prestige and position without God in the picture, working smart, and helping the upright poor. And he'll sprinkle in a little whining here and there to see if you've learned patience with people who can be a bit frustrating from time to time—that's part of wisdom too. It's available to us, so dig in wholeheartedly, prayerfully, expectantly. You won't be disappointed.

 Read Ecclesiastes 4:1–3.

OPTIONAL

**Memorize
Proverbs 31:30–31**
Charm is deceptive, and beauty is fleeting; but a woman who fears the LORD is to be praised. Honor her for all that her hands have done, and let her works bring her praise at the city gate.

1. Solomon looked at the common people and his heart ached for many of them. Why (4:1)? What makes your heart ache for others?

God desires to shine light into the dark places of injustice, and he does that through us.
—Gary Haugen (*Just Courage*, 65)

2. Does God share Solomon's concern? Discuss the verses below.

Psalm 12:5, 7–8

Psalm 72:12–14

Luke 4:14–21

DIGGING DEEPER

Psalm 72 is accredited to Solomon. Read and then wring out this psalm. What do you learn about the kind of king he wanted to be?

3. History records that later in his reign Solomon forced the common men in his kingdom to leave their jobs and families to work on his massive building projects (1 Kings 11:28; 12:4). How does this square with 4:1? What do you learn and what's the warning for us?

4. What was Solomon's depressed conclusion about the upright poor (4:2–3)?

5. Instead of moaning and giving up hope, what does God want us to do (Psalm 82:3–4; Isaiah 1:17)? What are some helpful ways to do that without harming the dignity of people who legitimately need our help?

 Read Ecclesiastes 4:4–6.

WORK WISELY

6. What else upsets Solomon (4:4)? Is this always true? What assumptions is he making about everyone's motivation to achieve?

A heart at peace gives life to the body, but envy rots the bones.
—Proverbs 14:30

Jealousy and envy are emotions we all feel from time to time. But if they are allowed to become dominant in our lives, they warp our perspectives, keep us from realizing our personal potential and . . . lead us into destructive behavior. Without question, jealousy and envy impede our growth to spiritual maturity.
—Vickie Kraft (*Facing Your Feelings*, 121)

7. Do you tend to jump to conclusions when you are irritated? Why is this foolish?

8. What correct assessments does Solomon make about work (vv. 5– 6)? How might "folding your hands" lead to poverty? What principles can you glean in these verses that will add beauty to your life right now?

 Read Ecclesiastes 4:7–12.

ONE IS THE LONELIEST NUMBER

9. What else upsets Solomon (4:8)? What lessons can we learn from this Scrooge-like character?

10. After Solomon describes this miserable lonely miser, he paints a word picture of the beautiful advantages of companionship and community (4:9–12). List the benefits. What personal examples of these benefits can you share with the group?

11. Do you see yourself or anyone you know (no names, please) in 4:8? What lessons should we take to heart to heighten our contentment and add to the richness of our daily lives?

12. We were made for community. Share some of the struggles you've experienced, past or present, in trying to become part of a group or community. If you feel included in a community, how can you reach out and offer the same blessing to others?

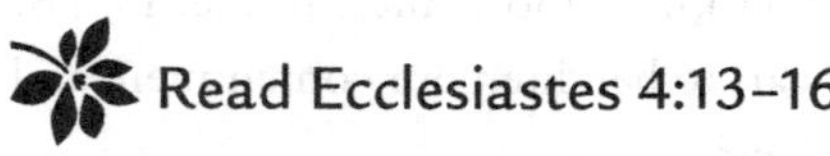 Read Ecclesiastes 4:13–16.

PRESTIGE AND POSITION WITHOUT GOD

This journal entry takes on a personal flare, making one wonder if the king is grappling with related political issues himself.

13. Describe what seems to be going on in 4:13–16. What ultimately happened to both the king and his successor?

14. Any thoughts on what Solomon might be trying to teach us? Although none of us are kings or kings' successors, what lessons might we glean for our lives today?

 Read Ecclesiastes 5:1–7.

WARNINGS ON WORSHIP

Solomon begins chapter 5 with somber warnings on worship. He reminds us to stand in awe of a holy God and to be careful as we come to the house of God that we don't offend him with meaningless rituals and false worship. "Come to God," he tells us, "but never try to use him."

15. Read Matthew 6:7 and 15:7–9. How do Jesus's words in these passages relate to Ecclesiastes 5:1–3?

16. Evaluate your heart attitude the last time you went to the house of God to worship. Did you spend more time listening, learning, and worshipping? Or visiting, talking, and criticizing? How might you make your time in the house of God more pleasing to him?

17. A vow is a religious promise—either positive, to do something, or negative, not to do something. In Old Testament times, people were never obliged to make a vow, but once they did, they were required to fulfill it (5:4–7). What did Jesus teach about vows (Matthew 5:33–37)?

Why is it important that your yes be yes and your no be no?

What happens in a culture when a person's word can no longer be trusted?

 **Read Ecclesiastes 5:8–17.**

POLITICS AND MONEY WITHOUT GOD IN THE PICTURE

(Please do not discuss political specifics. It's likely to cause division in your group.)

18. In 5:8 and 9, the author tells us not to be surprised when we see the love of money corrupting government officials. When will those who love money be satisfied (5:10)? Do you know anyone whose income is more than sufficient yet they always want more? (No names, please.) Any thoughts about why?

19. What are some of the problems and frustrations of people who pursue wealth as their primary goal in life (5:11–15)?

DIGGING DEEPER

Paul instructed Timothy concerning what to teach Christians about money in 1 Timothy 6:3–10 and 17–19. What are the lessons for us today?

Discontentment is an emotion that is capable of dwarfing us spiritually because it is directed against the Lord. If we are discontented with His will for us, then we're not going to grow in our faith.
—Vickie Kraft (*Facing Your Feelings*, 196)

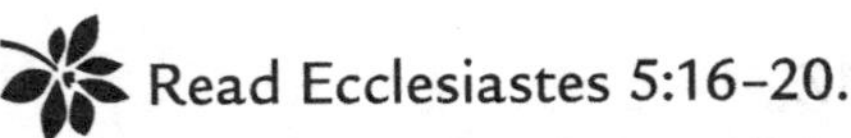 Read Ecclesiastes 5:16–20.

THE "BE HAPPY AND DO GOOD" REFRAIN

20. Solomon's words reflect a weary song in his soul in 5:16–17, but he quickly changes his tune in verses 18–20. Briefly summarize his realization. What additional insight does verse 20 provide?

 Read Ecclesiastes 6:1–12.

WHINING, WHINING, WHINING (ENOUGH ALREADY!)

21. For many people "under the sun," accumulating wealth is extremely important. But what often happens (6:1–6)? Would adding years to a person's lifespan solve the problem?

22. List some of the disappointments Solomon whines about in 6:7–12. Can you relate to any of them in your life today? If so, which ones? Why do they bug you?

23. In 6:7–12, again Solomon expresses frustration that all these things he has tried haven't resulted in satisfaction or joy. Can you relate to any of his frustrations? Below are some questions that might help you identify the source of your frustration:

Are you anxious because you are in debt?
Do you have too many things to care for?
Would you rather go shopping than spend time with God?
Are you disappointed with how quickly new possessions lose their appeal?
Are you sick of proper etiquette expectations?
Are you overwhelmed with information overload?
Are you irritated that life isn't fair?

These are questions we each need to ask ourselves from time to time. Discuss your related struggles and victories. How might God set you free?

If you're a little sick of Solomon's whining, you'll be glad to know that the next lesson is loaded with proverbs—wise sayings that teach us how to live with God in the picture.

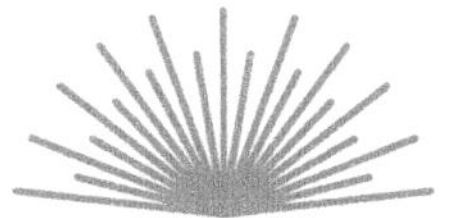

Choices Matter | LESSON 6

Every day we make hundreds of decisions. Many are so simple we make them without thinking. We've made those decisions before and we know the projected outcomes. Others involve unknown outcomes that are so serious they ultimately lead us in directions that change our lives forever. Dr. Alice Mathews writes, "Decisions. We make them. Then they turn around and make us. Sometimes they break us" (*Woman God Can Lead*, 3).

When God created us, he gave us the gift of free will, the ability to choose for ourselves. It's a precious endowment, separating us from automatons and giving us some power over our lives. We can choose to be lazy or work hard. We can choose to develop our minds or let them atrophy. We can choose to treat people well or be self-absorbed, and we can choose to love God or reject him.

Yes, we have predispositions to tendencies and addictions. Our families of origin and the neighborhoods where we grow up influence us. But remarkably, two children growing up in the same dysfunctional family and the same abusive neighborhood often make completely different choices in life. One may fall "victim" to those forces, while the other overcomes them, insisting, "I'll never live that way or treat others that way—I'm taking a different path!" We really do have choices.

Have you given serious thought to how you make choices?

- Are you quick to follow the latest fad?
- If a salesman pressures you to try his product, are you swift to cave?
- Do you dislike decision-making so much that you typically let others dictate the restaurant, movie, or vacation spot?
- Are you so indecisive that you frustrate loved ones?
- Do you care so much about what others think that you make choices just to please them?
- Do you make choices on the basis of quick or long-term results?

Becoming skilled at making wise choices is a lengthy process. My mother didn't allow me to make my own choices growing up so I entered adulthood unprepared, feeling unable to make good decisions. The result—six years of learning things the hard way, experiencing depression, and ending up miserable. But I sought help and God rescued me. He showed me that, with his help, I could choose wisely, and those choices made a dramatic difference in the course of my life.

Choices matter. Some result in good outcomes and others bad. It's foolish to say, "That may be true for you but that doesn't mean it's true for me." God showed me that there is truth and there are falsehoods, regardless of what the culture says. I searched and tested Scripture to see if what it suggested resulted in good outcomes or bad. At every turn, I found the Bible to be trustworthy. And I learned that a wise choice made on top of another wise choice and then another ultimately determines where we end up—in harmony with God, ourselves, and others, despite circumstances. The Bible offers God's good choices, available to us all. Taste and see that the Lord is good.

The journal entries featured in Lesson 6 teach us more about wise choices than any of Solomon's former entries. We discover them in the form of proverbs—short, pithy sayings that reflect the way the world works and how to live wisely in it. Scholars label books like Ecclesiastes, Proverbs, and Song of Songs *wisdom literature*—divine writings given by God to teach us how to live skillfully every day as we face different experiences and problems, necessitating various choices. We are wise when we know how to respond biblically to whatever comes our way.

Solomon continues to vacillate between wise and skewed thinking, just not as much. I'll indicate when I think he's reverting to depressed, perverted thinking to help you distinguish between the two.

The meanings of some of these proverbs may initially seem obscure. Do the best you can. I'll help by adding notes to reflect the thinking of respected scholars. Regardless of their difficulty, these sayings teach us valuable lessons expressed in unforgettable ways, so it's worth the work. And sharing insights in your group will probably be an additional help for everyone.

❋ *Choose sobriety; reject frivolity. Read 7:1–4.*

1. In what way might a house of mourning be better than a house of feasting?

What reality are we required to face at funerals? Although this is unpleasant, why is it good to look this square in the face?

In what way is a sad face good for the heart?

When the perishable has been clothed with the imperishable, and the mortal with immortality, then the saying that is written will come true: "Death has been swallowed up in victory." "Where, O death, is your victory? Where, O death, is your sting?" The sting of death is sin, and the power of sin is the law. But thanks be to God! He gives us the victory through our Lord Jesus Christ.

—Paul's words in 1 Corinthians 15:54–57

Precious in the sight of the LORD is the death of his faithful servants.

—Psalm 116:15

DIGGING DEEPER

Have you considered your future death? Death is not a favorite topic of conversation but every day the news reports a tragedy that unexpectedly takes the lives of innocent people, whether godly or ungodly. Psalm 89:48 asks, "Who can live and not see death, or who can escape the power of the grave?" Do you want to be prepared with hope? Read Isaiah 57:2, Hebrews 2:12–15, 1 Corinthians 15:54–57, 1 Thessalonians 4:13–14, and Revelation 21:1–4. What does God promise you as you contemplate your own physical death?

2. In contrast, what is the atmosphere of a house of pleasure (banquet, dinner party)? What would a fool fail to learn there?

3. Any ideas why Solomon began these couplets with the proverb, "A good name is better than fine perfume"?

🌸 *Prize a rebuke; scorn flattery. Read 7:5–6.*

When Solomon compares the song of fools to the crackling of thorns under a pot, he's referring to the practice of burning dried thorn bushes when you need a small amount of quick heat.

4. Which is more pleasant to hear—correction or flattery? Which is likely to do us more good? Why?

5. What is the difference between flattery and encouragement?

6. What is usually your first response when someone corrects you? Share your struggles or victories when dealing with correction.

❋ *Be patient; control your anger. Read 7:8–9.*

7. Why might the end of a matter be better than its beginning? Have you ever overreacted to a situation only to find that it didn't turn out nearly so bad as you had envisioned?

8. Why do you think patience, or forbearance, is one of the fruits of the Spirit (Galatians 5:22)?

9. What situations typically "try your patience" or even end with you exploding in anger? If you have learned patience, share how with the group.

10. What do you think is the relationship between anger (7:9) and pride (7:8)?

 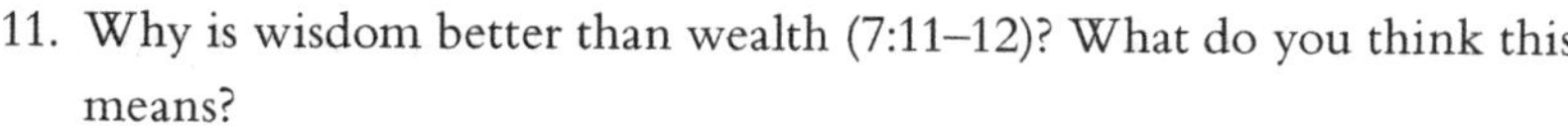

❉ *Accept God's ways; don't complain. Read 7:10–14.*

11. Why is wisdom better than wealth (7:11–12)? What do you think this means?

Would you rather be wise than rich? Why or why not?

12. Wise people know how to respond in both good and bad times. What is their attitude in each? Why do they feel this way (7:13–14)?

This reorientation to the ultimate reality of God's love and goodness is an important first step to receiving guidance. For only when we know the love of God in a deep, experiential way can we be truly open and receptive to his will. Without this knowing it is hard to listen openly for the still, small voice of God, because we are afraid of what we may hear.
—Ruth Haley Barton
(*Invitation to Solitude*, 116)

13. What helps us trust God whether he is showering us with blessings or taking them away? Consider the New Testament perspectives in Romans 8:28–30, Galatians 6:9, and John 9:1–3. Add any of your own reasons.

Note on 7:15–19. On the surface these verses seem confusing, but scholars shed light on Solomon's possible intentions. For example, Garrett argues that Solomon is warning readers against a pathological "religion" that links obedience and self-righteousness with guaranteed prosperity and long life. He's observed too many exceptions in his lifetime. The "overrighteous" and "overwise" cannot escape adversity (7:16). Neither can we conclude that a sinful life reaps no consequences (7:17). The bottom line seems to be found in verse 18 where the wise person is counseled to avoid all extremes. They will understand that no one in this life can completely overcome sin, nor can we completely understand the details of what God is doing. Thus the wise person learns to revere God, trusting that he knows what he's doing. (See Garrett, *Proverbs, Ecclesiastes, Song of Songs*, 323–24; see also Constable, *Notes*, 34–35.)

❋ *Exercise self-restraint; reject impulsive reactions. Read 7:20–22.*

14. What is the main lesson Solomon wants to teach us in these verses? Why should wise people be tolerant of others?

15. If you fail to heed his advice, what problems might you encounter in life?

I am the vine; you are the branches. If you remain in me and I in you, you will bear much fruit; apart from me you can do nothing.
—Jesus's words in John 15:5

❋ *Embrace God's truth; renounce faith in human wisdom. Read 7:23–8:1.*

As you read, remember Solomon's admonition to *be patient* and to *control your anger.*

16. Solomon was known throughout the ancient world as a very wise and learned scholar. With that in mind, what is the significance of his statements in 7:23–24 and 8:1?

17. Solomon tried to "search out wisdom and the scheme of things" without God's guidance (7:25). He came to several different conclusions about life (7:26, 28–29)—some true and others distorted. Which do you think are true and which are distorted?

 *Be respectful; not rebellious. Read 8:2–8.*

Although these words originally applied to the subjects' relationship with their king, we can glean some principles for working with bosses and those in authority over us.

18. What advice does Solomon give us regarding our attitude and actions toward those in authority?

19. Look back over the kinds of choices Solomon has counseled you to make in this lesson. Pick at least one that pertains to your life right now and determine a wiser course of action than your typical response in the past. Be specific. For accountability, if you would like, share your wiser way of responding with your group and try it out this week.

20. Envision yourself ten years from now as a wise woman—a woman who knows God's Word, takes it to heart, and has applied it faithfully over this time span. Describe what you see. God wants this picture to become reality just as much as you do. What would it take on your part to get there?

I shall be telling this
  with a sigh
Somewhere ages and
  ages hence:
Two roads diverged in
  a wood, and I—
I took the one less
  traveled by,
And that has made all
  the difference.
    —Robert Frost, from
    "The Road Not Taken"

Find Purpose and Joy in an Unpredictable World

"I just want to be happy." When I served as a minister to women in my church, I heard these words often. As a seminary professor I still hear them occasionally. I try to help women understand that experiencing satisfaction in life cannot be our primary goal. It's a by-product of living a life of purpose, and even then, it's impacted by the reality that we live in a corrupted, fallen world where mosquitoes carry deadly viruses and tornadoes destroy.

I also try to explain the difference between joy and happiness, a useful contrast as we work our way through this lesson's journal entries (8:9–10:1). That's because two of Ecclesiastes' refrains about enjoying life are included in this section:

> So I commend the enjoyment of life, because there is nothing better for a person under the sun than to eat and drink and be glad. Then joy will accompany them in their toil all the days of the life God has given them under the sun. (8:15)

> Go, eat your food with gladness, and drink your wine with a joyful heart, for God has already approved what you do. Always be clothed in white, and always anoint your head with oil. Enjoy life with your wife, whom you love, all the days of this meaningless [fleeting] life that God has given you under the sun. . . . Whatever your hand finds to do, do it with all your might. (9:7–10).

Notice that Solomon uses the word enjoyment rather than happiness. That's because happiness depends on what happens. We experience happiness when life goes our way. We look forward to something we like to do. The day looks promising, we're laughing and having fun, and then, like a flash: a flat tire, a sick child, a bad-news phone call—the smile fades, the heart is disappointed, and happiness wanes. Happiness is related to circumstances, but joy isn't.

It's impossible to be happy all the time. We all face struggles and misfortune, but joy can abide. Joy is the second fruit of the Spirit (Galatians 5:22) and it's a gift of God, independent of circumstances.

Here's a picture that expresses the true meaning of joy: Ocean gales rip across the Pacific and can catapult waves fifty feet high. Yet fifty feet below the surface the water is calm and serene. Happiness is like the surface of the sea, chaotic and ever changing. Joy is like the ocean bed, peaceful and ever the same. Joy is the abiding presence of God's Spirit deep down inside, a foretaste of that face-to-face communion with God that will blossom in eternity.

God delights in giving you the gift of joy, as you'll see clearly in this week's passages. And joy is possible regardless of the circumstances we face. It's healthy to work through difficulties, expecting in time that joy will emerge as we give our situations to our loving heavenly Father.

It's my prayer, fervent hope, and expectation that this lesson will help you reframe your thinking about the difference between happiness and joy, and you'll realize that joy is a by-product of living a life of purpose, all God's gift to you because he's good and because he loves you.

 **Read Ecclesiastes 8:9–15.**

WHERE'S THE JUDGE?

1. In these verses, Solomon observes people oppressing and taking advantage of others (8:9). Yet so often, these wicked people mingle with honorable people as if they were one of them. Even when they die, they are buried with honor (8:10). Without specific names, what similar situations can we observe in our society today?

2. What is one reason that injustice thrives both then and now (8:11; Romans 3:10, 23–26)?

3. Compare 8:14 with 3:17. Is there justice "under the sun"? Will justice ever be carried out? What does Solomon conclude in 8:12–13?

4. In what sense will it go better with people who "fear God"? (See Psalm 37:1, 6–11.)

5. Are you allowing the reality of injustice in the world to discourage or hinder you from the joyous and productive life God wants for you? If so, how might you overcome these obstacles and live out God's purposes instead?

6. List Solomon's suggestions for a simple but joyous life in 8:15 and 9:7–9 and the first part of verse 10. (Note: Since bleach and other stain removers were not available, wearing white and anointing oneself with perfumed oils was reserved for special occasions.)

7. What do you think Paul, as a New Testament apostle, might add to Solomon's list? Consider the following passages. From your own experiences, what else would you add to the list?

Galatians 2:20

Galatians 5:1

Philippians 4:6–7

Philippians 4:11–13

You can see God from anywhere if your mind is set to love and obey Him. . . . When the habit of inwardly gazing Godward becomes fixed within us, we shall be ushered onto a new level of spiritual life more in keeping with the promises of God and the mood of the New Testament. The Triune God will be our dwelling place even while our feet walk the low road of simple duty here among men.

—A. W. Tozer (*Pursuit of God*, 88-90)

8. What's hindering you from enjoying a simple but joyous life today?

Read Ecclesiastes 8:16–9:12.

One of the disturbing aspects of life is the fact that so many things are beyond our understanding and control. In these verses, Solomon wrestles with many of life's perplexities and contradictions. Again, he vacillates between a godly perspective and a distorted perspective.

9. What are some of the observations this frustrated skeptic makes from his distorted perspective (9:2–6, 11–12)?

What similar words have come out of your mouth as you experienced life "under the sun"?

DIGGING DEEPER

Scholars disagree on whether or not Christians will receive different rewards in Christ's kingdom. Passages like 2 Corinthians 5:10 say that believers will appear before the *bema* seat to receive what is due them "while in the body, whether good or bad." The *bema* seat was the place where Olympic athletes received their particular rewards or honors according to their placements in winning the contests. Related texts include Revelation 22:5 and 12, Luke 19:11–26, Matthew 20:1–16, and 1 Corinthians 3:10–15. Write an essay either supporting the view that believers will receive different rewards after death or against this view. Support your ideas with Scripture.

10. Solomon claims in 9:5 that the dead have no further reward. But is this true? Consider the following passages in response: John 3:16; Jude 20–21; Romans 6:23; 1 John 5:11–12; 2 Corinthians 5:1–10. Can you think of other passages to add to this discussion?

 Read Ecclesiastes 9:13–10:1.

THE DIFFERENCE ONE PERSON CAN MAKE

11. What effect can a poor but wise person have on the world around them (9:14–15, 17)?

12. What effect can one sinner have on their world (9:18; 10:1)? What
    examples come to mind?

13. Why do you think the people of the city were so ungrateful (9:15–16)?
    Can the wise expect to be appreciated?

14. Read Luke 17:11–19. Briefly, what happened? Put yourself in the shoes
    of those who were healed. What do you think your response would
    have been? Why do you think gratitude is rare, both then and now?

15. How does this influence your motivation to serve God and do good in the world, even if it is unjust and people are seldom thankful?

16. How much good can a wise person do if they don't care who gets the credit? What good is God calling you to do right now? What impact can you have on the world around you? Are you listening or resisting? If the latter, what do you need to do to equip yourself and get going?

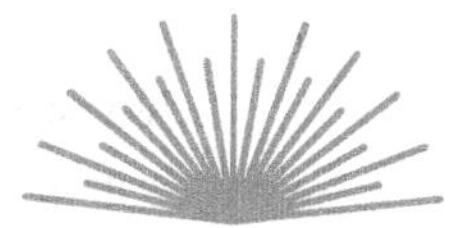

Are You Judgmental or Are You Discerning?

OPTIONAL

**Memorize
Proverbs 11:22**
Like a gold ring in a pig's snout is a beautiful woman who shows no discretion.

Despite the reality that we cannot know exactly what God is doing, we can attain timeless wisdom and live skillfully in our everyday lives. This lesson is jam-packed with wisdom principles on various topics. Take them in. Wring them out. Don't water-ski over them, as is the habit of the careless student. If you take your time, meditate thoughtfully on the words and meanings, and consider how to apply them to your world and specific circumstances, they will serve you well.

Most of the lesson paints a stark contrast between fools who live as if God did not exist, and wise people who include God in the picture. Solomon shows us how to live with purpose, so we won't end up spouting his mantra, "Meaningless! Meaningless! Utterly Meaningless! Without God everything is meaningless." Although it's true that we must patiently await God's judgment on fools, Solomon assures us that we can trust God to ultimately vindicate us if we love him, serve him, and attempt to walk in his ways.

To glean Solomon's meanings from several of the proverbs in this lesson, realize that when he refers to fools and slaves he's not referring so much to their social status as he is to their assumed moral character, and, from his perspective, it is lacking. And when he refers to the rich and to princes, he sees them as people to be admired—people of noble character.

Throughout Ecclesiastes we are instructed to discern foolish actions and attitudes from wise ones. But to be discerning, we must make value judgments about other people's actions and attitudes. Our culture blares, "Tolerance is the highest virtue. What's right for you may not be right for me, and you cannot say that I'm wrong." It's easy to acquiesce to these demands. Otherwise we might appear intolerant and even mean-spirited. But the Bible affirms that truth is real, and if there is truth, then there is falsehood. If there's a wise way to live there's also a foolish way to live.

In this lesson, we'll grapple with the question: How do I live as a wise, discerning Christian without becoming a hyper-judgmental Pharisee in my attitudes and actions? How do I exhibit the gracious heart of Jesus while I live and speak the truth in love, as instructed in Ephesians 4:15?

Wrestling with the distinction between developing a discerning spirit and a judgmental attitude is the task of all-in Jesus followers, and it's particularly important in the twenty-first–century culture where tolerance is such a high value. We must learn to navigate the tensions brought on by these issues. It's made worse because the two terms, discernment and judgment, are sometimes used interchangeably, but if we look closely, we see that they have different meanings.

Before we begin our study of Ecclesiastes 10:2–11:6, we need to understand the differences between a judgmental spirit and a discerning spirit. Some of us fail to distinguish between the two, which produces serious consequence because the Bible prohibits being judgmental and encourages being discerning.

Let's begin by looking carefully at these definitions, derived from various dictionaries:

> **Discernment**: a keenness of insight; the power to detect; the ability to see or understand subtle differences; the quality of being able to grasp and comprehend what is obscure; accuracy in perception, such as in reading character or motives

> **Judgment**: the ability to make a decision or form an opinion objectively, authoritatively, and wisely; a formal utterance of an authoritative opinion; a formal decision given by a court; the determination by God of the ultimate worthiness and destiny of all individuals; a divine sentence or decision

1. By looking closely at the definitions, what differences and subtle nuances can you glean between these two words, discernment and judgment?

2. Read Matthew 7:1–6. In Jesus's great Sermon on the Mount contrasting true God followers with the religious leaders of the day, he taught his followers wisdom principles about judging others. He warned them not to adopt the Pharisees' harsh, self-righteous, judgmental attitudes. What is the warning in 7:1?

In light of the definitions on page 90, what kind of judging do you think Jesus is talking about? Why?

What would help Christians maintain a humble spirit when they discern actions and attitudes of others (7:3–5)?

When am I being judgmental and when am I being discerning and then called to rebuke sin? The rebuke does not mean to point out every sin we see; it means to bring sin to a person's attention with the purpose of restoring him or her to God and to fellow humans. When you feel you must rebuke another Christian for a sin, check your attitude before you speak. Do you love the person? Are you willing to forgive? Unless rebuke is tied to forgiveness, it will not help the sinning person.
—*Life Application Study Bible* notes (p. 1840)

Both dogs and pigs were despised in the time of Christ. What was Jesus's advice concerning when to witness to people about him and what kinds of results to expect (7:6)?

Think of a time you watched a woman respond to a situation with keen insight. She was able to read the character and attitudes of people involved, and distinguish shades of meaning beyond the obvious. She detected what was really going on, and understood what was true from what was false, right from wrong. Then she responded with wise choices and sound judgment.

Would you like to be a woman who knows how to navigate her way in the world? We call her mature. The Bible calls her wise, discerning, and discreet. Discretion is discernment in action. We all admire women like this. Some of us think this is a special gift, inaccessible to ordinary people. We are wrong. It is God's desire and design that we all be discerning women who live discreet lives. Only through following Christ can we actually become that woman! —Sue

DIGGING DEEPER

Abigail is an excellent model of a discerning woman who exhibited discreet behavior that saved lives. Study 1 Samuel 25 and analyze the character of this outstanding woman.

3. What does Paul pray for the Philippians in Philippians 1:9–11? What will result? Does God desire and expect that all his children will develop a discerning spirit?

OLD TESTAMENT INSIGHTS INTO JUDGING AND DISCERNING

4. As a youth about to become king over Israel, what did Solomon ask God (1 Kings 3:9)? What would that enable him to do?

5. Solomon's book of Proverbs reveals God's strong desire that we all become discerning women as a prerequisite for being wise. What do you learn from the sampling below?

3:21

14:6

14:33

17:24

PERSONAL ASSESSMENT AND APPLICATION

6. Do you struggle with a judgmental spirit when others don't live up to your expectations? Describe a time when your judgmental attitude or actions did not turn out for the good of others or the glory of God. How might the results have been different if you had displayed a discerning spirit instead?

7. Have you ever said, "We must not judge," when faced with a difficult situation where the Lord was probably calling you to be discerning, and as a result you did not respond wisely? Do you tend to use Jesus's words in Matthew 7:1 as an excuse not to evaluate inappropriate or sinful behavior in others? Share specifics, if you are comfortable. (No names, please.)

8. What have you learned that might help others in your group respond with discernment rather than judgment? Should Christians respond differently to Christians than they should to nonbelievers? What are some wise ways to assess situations with a discerning heart that will ultimately be more likely to turn others to Jesus rather than away from him?

Keep in mind what you have learned about distinguishing between discernment and judgment as you study this lesson's text in Ecclesiastes. Here Solomon records a series of proverbs, those wise sayings that teach us biblical wisdom, skill in living.

 Read Ecclesiastes 10.

LESSONS FROM SOLOMON

9. According to Ecclesiastes 10:2–3, 15, what are some qualities you can look for to discern if someone exhibits foolish attitudes and actions (see also Proverbs 13:16)? Why do you think Solomon is asking you to assess the behavior of a fool?

Ecclesiastes 10:4–7, 16–17, 20 pertain to politics and wise leadership from Solomon's perspective, a king who lived almost three thousand years ago. In those days nations were ruled by monarchs and only the wealthier class enjoyed the privilege of an education. Keep these realities in mind as you interpret these proverbs and apply them today. (Remember, no divisive political discussions, please.) Note: To feast in the morning (v. 16) was considered foolish and inappropriate.

10. What is Solomon's advice if someone in authority is angry with you (10:4)? Have you ever found yourself in this situation? If so, what did you learn?

Through patience a ruler can be persuaded, and a gentle tongue can break a bone.
—Proverbs 25:15

11. What does Solomon think of leaders who put unprepared people in influential positions in government (10:5–7)? How do these decisions affect the nations (10:16–17)?

12. What often results when leaders aren't prepared for the offices they are holding or work for a boss who is incompetent? (No names, please.) How do you feel about these kinds of situations?

13. What is the warning in 10:20? What colloquialism from these verses has been passed down through the ages?

14. The following verses deal with saving time and working smarter. What wisdom principle is contained in each?

10:8–9

10:10

10:11

15. Saving time and working smarter afford more time to spend on other worthwhile endeavors. What related wisdom principles have you discovered that might be helpful to the women in your group?

16. What impresses you about the tongue in 10:12–14?

"I just didn't have enough time." Yes you did. You had all the time there is. You had the same twenty-four hours, the same 1,440 minutes, that everyone else did. But you didn't have the skills of managing the time that was available to you.
—Alec Mackenzie
(*Time Trap*, 3)

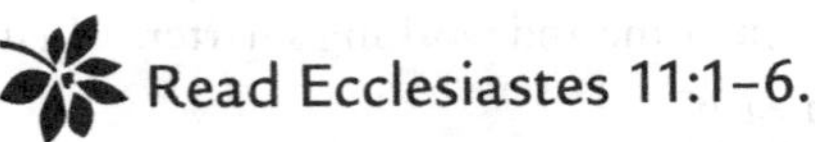
Read Ecclesiastes 11:1–6.

"Cast your bread upon the waters" or "ship your grain across the sea" (11:1) exhorts us to work hard and give generously and charitably in a variety of ways. This passage could apply to sharing our time, money, or faith.

17. Verse 4 counsels us not to hold back too cautiously, waiting for conditions to be perfect before we give or invest. What illustrations from nature does Solomon use to teach this lesson?

18. What happens to the person who waits until all conditions are "just right" to work, to give, to serve, to witness (10:4)?

Giving to the Lord for the expansion of His kingdom breaks the iron grip money can have on our hearts. When we give, it increases our faith because we experience the effect our generosity has on others. They thank God for what He has used us to do. This stimulates us to more generosity and helps make us good role models for other believers. It's always faith-building to see the many ways God has of replenishing our supply.
—Vickie Kraft (*Facing Your Feelings*, 151)

19. What does verse 5 tell us about God? How do you think this verse relates to the entire passage (10:1–6)?

20. Solomon tells us to work hard, invest with the knowledge we have, and do the best we can because we can't know for certain what will happen. While this is true, what does Paul add that is also true (1 Corinthians 15:58)?

21. Look back over the proverbs in this lesson. What new truths have you learned? How do you think God wants you to apply this lesson to your life right now? What could you change in your attitude or actions this week that would put you on the road to wiser living?

The Final Journal Entry—Wisdom for Our Last Days

Solomon concludes his journal first with rich insight for younger women, charging them to enjoy their youth instead of practicing the typical ritual of morning body hatred: *my hips are too flabby, my stomach's too saggy, I found a wrinkle on my face and a gray hair on my chin.* Honestly, it makes me want to say, *Stop it—you are beautiful. Enjoy.* Sometimes I do.

Our author goes on with some honest commentary on aging—much of it from his skewed perspective "under the sun," although growing old is not for sissies and he's right on target if you want a realistic dose of what's ahead. Maybe a good dose of reality will wake up some of you younger women to enjoy the strength and health typical of younger years. It's good to realize that no matter how much you exercise or lather on the cream, in time your body will let you know that you weren't made to last forever. But if you know Christ, rejoice because you're leaving your earthly body behind one day and trading it for an eternal spiritual body. And, as the lesson proceeds, I'll add in more positive perspectives from other parts of the Bible to offset Solomon's gloomy approach.

He ends his journal with bottom-line wisdom for life that I think you'll find helpful. As we end our trek through Ecclesiastes together, I'm hopeful that God has given you rich insight into the big questions we all ask: What's the meaning of life? Who created all this? Why am I here? What's the best way to live out the years I've been given? Solomon warns us not to go down the paths he traveled "under the sun." We can bypass the pain he brought on himself and instead look up and follow the Son. Abundant life awaits you there. It's up to you. Make your life a worthy pursuit rather than ultimate futility.

Read Ecclesiastes 11:7–10.

Although we can glean valuable insight from parts of this last entry, we also see Solomon's cynical attitude peeking through from time to time.

OPTIONAL

Memorize Psalm 90:12
Teach us to number our days, that we may gain a heart of wisdom.

1. Throughout this essay, Solomon pictures the gradual aging process using a light and darkness motif. What does he say in 11:7 and the first part of verse 8? Do you agree?

2. What does he ask younger women to remember in the last part of 11:8 and 12:1?

3. Solomon takes a dim view of aging. In 2 Corinthians 4:16–18, Paul both agrees and disagrees with Solomon. Observe the passage and answer the following questions:

   How do Solomon's and Paul's tone compare and contrast as they write about aging?

What is happening to our physical bodies as we age? What is happening inwardly if we know, love, and walk with Christ? (v. 16)

Paul honestly admits that older years often come with some "light and momentary troubles" (v. 17), but what does he say they are achieving? What do you think he means?

How does Paul suggest we cope with any difficulties that accompany the aging process (v. 18)? What would that actually look like in an older person's life?

What might be some benefits of growing older? Do you know someone who illustrates these benefits? If so, describe them and why you admire them.

ADVICE TO THE YOUNG

4. Several times Solomon exhorts young people to enjoy life. How specifically does he command them to do that in 11:9–10? What do you think he means?

5. Did you learn to "banish anxiety from your heart and cast off the troubles of your body" (11:10) when you were still "young"? What are some ways to do that?

6. Why might it be good to learn to apply verse 10 in your youth, instead of when you are older? How can coming to Christ in your youth affect the rest of your life?

7. Solomon also cautions younger people. What is the warning in the last part of verse 9?

The Bible reveals two different kinds of judgment. The first is the judgment of believers before Christ's *bema* seat, named after the place where rewards were handed out at the original Olympic Games. "For we must all appear before the judgment seat of Christ, so that each of us may receive what is due us for the things done while in the body, whether good or bad" (2 Corinthians 5:10). This judgment does not determine our eternal destiny. That's already fixed because of what Jesus did for us on the cross. But these rewards will determine some aspect of our eternal life. The Bible also reveals the great white throne judgment (Revelation 20:11–15) which describes the eternal destiny of those who have not trusted in Christ for the forgiveness of their sins.

 Read Ecclesiastes 12:1–8.

If you read Lamentations 3:22–23, you will discover that God's love, compassion, and faithfulness will never fail you. What a relief to know God hears us (Jeremiah 33:3) when we call to him to spill out all our fears and worries. Remember the words of Psalm 46:10, "Be still, and know that I am God; I will be exalted among the nations, I will be exalted in the earth." As you journey through the valleys of your life, shine your light so that others see that you know God is trustworthy. The way to find relief from fear and anxiety is to seek calm and rest in his Word and his presence.

—Cynthia Hester, seminary intern

DIGGING DEEPER

Read Romans 8:18–25. According to these verses, is our struggle against futility real? Is it permanent? Describe the hope of Christians, even as they face old age and death.

8. In 12:2–7, we encounter the Bible's classic description of old age, written in figurative language. (Contemporary translations and paraphrases—such as the Living Bible, the Voice, or the New Living Translation—can help you with the symbolism.) What do you think the following images might represent?

Keepers of the house tremble

Strong men stoop

Grinders cease

Windows dim

Doors close

Sounds fade

People rise

People fear

Almond tree blossoms

Grasshopper drags

Desire ceases

Silver cord severed/golden bowl broken/pitcher shattered/wheel broken

9. What strikes you as the most personally challenging from these images?

GOD'S CALL TO THE AGED

10. Reconcile Solomon's picture of aging with the truths presented in Psalm 92:12–15 and Proverbs 20:29.

11. What is the special task of older people mentioned in Psalm 71:17–18? Why are they especially qualified for this opportunity? If you are "older" what avenues have you found to carry out this task?

12. What is the promise to the aged in Isaiah 46:4?

13. How might facing old age and a deteriorating physical body be easier for a Christian? Consider 1 Corinthians 15:42–44 and John 14:1–4.

14. Have you faced the reality that you are growing older and with age will probably come challenges? Share some of your fears or questions about aging. How do you think these years can best be faced positively?

In Ecclesiastes 12:8 Solomon restates the theme of his journal: Without God, everything ultimately proves to be empty and without real meaning. Has Solomon given you enough evidence that this statement is now a deep conviction of your mind and heart?

 Read Ecclesiastes 12:9–14.

15. In 12:9–10, Solomon gives us his credentials. Why does he say we should listen to him?

Solomon divides what he wrote into two categories: goads and nails (12:11). Review the definition of goads in the sidebar on page 51. The nails he's talking about are probably large stakes used to secure tents and keep them from blowing down in the wind.

16. Why do you think Solomon divides his various journal entries into these two different categories? In what way are parts of his journal "goads"? In what way are other parts "nails"?

17. What is the warning in verse 12? See also the warning at the conclusion of the Bible in Revelation 22:18–19. What are some of the ways
people have tried to add to or take away from the Scriptures? Why is
this so dangerous?

18. Through the ages many philosophers have written numerous books
that contradict one another. Why might a study of these and other
books "weary the body"? If you have experienced this, please share.

We've already studied about several of the key concepts in these final
verses: (1) the fear of God and (2) the coming evaluation of believers' lives
at the *bema* seat and the judgment for nonbelievers' lives at the great white
throne judgment. Nevertheless, reminders are always helpful.

19. Solomon concludes with a powerful exhortation. What is the bottom
line of life and the whole duty of all of us (12:13)?

20. How do the passages below shape our understanding of living out our "whole duty" according to our Savior Jesus Christ and the apostle Paul? (The author of Hebrews is unknown.)

Matthew 22:34–40

Galatians 5:6

Galatians 5:13–16

Hebrews 4:12

James 1:22–25

Synthesize these concepts into several concise sentences.

DIGGING DEEPER

What other passages could be added to the discussion in question 20? How do they further shape our understanding of living out our "whole duty"?

21. Glance back over your study of Ecclesiastes. What stands out that you think you'll remember a year from now?

22. When you meet Solomon in our eternal home, what would you like to ask him or say to him? How would you like to live differently in light of the messages in Solomon's journal? What are you going to do to make that desire a reality?

Works Cited

Augustine of Hippo. *The Confessions of St. Augustine, Bishop of Hippo.* Translated by J. G. Pilkington. Edinburgh: T&T Clark, 1876.

Barton, Ruth Haley. *Invitation to Solitude and Silence: Experiencing God's Transforming Presence.* Downers Grove, IL: InterVarsity Press, 2010.

Boa, Kenneth. "Wisdom." Leadership Qualities, Bible.org. November 4, 2005. https://bible.org/seriespage/14-wisdom.

Brestin, Dee. *Ecclesiastes: God's Wisdom for Evangelism.* Wheaton, IL: Harold Shaw Publishers, 1980.

Briscoe, Stuart, and Jill Briscoe. *Improving with Age: God's Plan for Getting Older and Better.* Fort Washington, PA: CLC Publications, 2015.

Chan, Francis. *Crazy Love: Overwhelmed by a Relentless God.* Colorado Springs: David C. Cook, 2008.

Constable, Tom. *Notes on Ecclesiastes.* Sonic Light. 2017 edition. http://www.soniclight.com/constable/notes/pdf/ecclesiastes.pdf.

Dyer, John. *From the Garden to the City: The Redeeming and Corrupting Power of Technology.* Grand Rapids: Kregel, 2011.

Edwards, Sue, and Kelley Mathews. *Leading Women Who Wound: Strategies for an Effective Ministry.* Chicago: Moody Press, 2009.

Edwards, Sue, and Barbara Neumann. *Organic Mentoring: A Mentor's Guide to Relationships with Next Generation Women.* Grand Rapids: Kregel, 2014.

Foster, Richard. *Celebration of Discipline: The Path to Spiritual Growth.* New York: HarperCollins, 1998.

Foxe's Book of Martyrs: Updated Through the Centuries to the Present Day, by John Foxe. Edited by Harold J. Chadwick. Alachua, FL: Bridge-Logos, 2001.

Garrett, Duane A. *Proverbs, Ecclesiastes, Song of Songs.* The New American Commentary: An Exegetical and Theological Exposition of Holy Scripture 14. Nashville: Broadman Press, 2002.

Glenn, Donald R. "Ecclesiastes" in *The Bible Knowledge Commentary: Old Testament.* Vol. 1. Edited by John F. Walvoord and Roy B. Zuck. Wheaton, IL: Victor Books, 1985.

Gorman, Julie A. *Community That Is Christian: A Handbook on Small Groups.* Grand Rapids: Baker, 2002.

Graham, Billy. *The Secret of Happiness.* Nashville: Thomas Nelson, 2002.

Haugen, Gary A. *Just Courage: God's Great Expedition for the Restless Christian.* Downers Grove, IL: InterVarsity Press, 2008.

Hendricks, Howard G., and William D. Hendricks. *Living by the Book.* Chicago: Moody Press, 1991.

Hengstenberg, Ernst W. *Commentary on Ecclesiastes, with Other Treatises.* New York: Smith, English, and Co., 1860.

James, Carolyn Custis. *Half the Church: Recapturing God's Global Vision for Women.* Grand Rapids: Zondervan, 2011.

Jensen, Irving L. *Ecclesiastes and Song of Solomon: A Self-Study Guide.* Chicago: Moody Press, 1974.

Kaiser, Walter C., Jr. *Ecclesiastes: Total Life.* Chicago: Moody Press, 1979.

Kraft, Vickie. *Facing Your Feelings: Moving from Emotional Bondage to Spiritual Freedom.* Dallas: Word Publishing, 1996.

Lewis, C. S. *Problem of Pain.* London: Collins Publishers, 1962.

Life Application Study Bible. Wheaton, IL: Tyndale House Publishers, 1991.

Lockyer, Herbert, Sr. Foreword to *The Pursuit of Holiness*, by Jerry Bridges. Colorado Springs: NavPress, 1978.

MacArthur, John. *The MacArthur Bible Handbook.* Nashville: Thomas Nelson, 2003.

Mackenzie, Alec. *The Time Trap: The Classic Book on Time Management.* 3rd edition. New York: American Management Association, 1997.

Mathews, Alice. *A Woman God Can Lead.* Grand Rapids: Discovery House Publishers, 1998.

Myers, Warren, and Ruth Myers. *Praise: A Door to God's Presence.* Colorado Springs: NavPress, 1987.

Ortlund, Anne. *Up with Worship: How to Quit Playing Church.* Ventura, CA: Regal Books, 1975.

Peck, M. Scott. *The Different Drum: Community Making and Peace.* New York: Simon & Schuster, 1987.

Perry, Ralph Barton. *The Thought and Character of William James.* Vol. 2. Boston: Little, Brown, and Co., 1935.

Reeve, Pamela. *Parables of the Vineyard.* Sisters, OR: Multnomah, 2004.

Spurgeon, Charles. *Evening by Evening.* New York: Sheldon and Company, 1869.

Swindoll, Charles R. *Living on the Ragged Edge: Coming to Terms with Reality.* Waco, TX: Word Books, 1985.

———. *Three Steps Forward, Two Steps Back.* Nashville: Thomas Nelson, 1980.

Tenney, Merrill C., ed. *The Zondervan Pictorial Bible Dictionary.* Grand Rapids: Zondervan, 1967.

Tozer, A. W. *The Pursuit of God: The Human Thirst for the Divine.* Camp Hill, PA: WingSpread Publishers, 2007.

Trotter, I. Lilias. *Parables of the Cross*. North Charleston, SC: CreateSpace, 2017.

Unger, Merrill F. *The New Unger's Bible Dictionary*. Rev. ed. Edited by R. K. Harrison. Chicago: Moody Press, 1988.

Unice, Nicole. *She's Got Issues: Seriously Good News for Stressed-Out, Secretly Scared Control Freaks Like Us*. Carol Stream, IL: Tyndale House Publishers, 2012.

Voskamp, Ann. *One Thousand Gifts*. Grand Rapids: Zondervan, 2010.

White, John. *The Golden Cow: Materialism in the Twentieth-Century Church*. Downers Grove, IL: InterVarsity Press, 1979.

About the Author

Sue Edwards is associate professor of educational ministries and leadership (her specialization is women's studies) at Dallas Theological Seminary, where she has the opportunity to equip men and women for future ministry. She brings over forty years of experience into the classroom as a Bible teacher, curriculum writer, and overseer of several megachurch women's ministries. As minister to women at Irving Bible Church and director of women's ministry at Prestonwood Baptist Church in Dallas, she has worked with women from all walks of life, ages, and stages. Her passion is to see modern and postmodern women connect, learn from one another, and bond around God's Word. Her Bible studies have ushered thousands of women all over the country and overseas into deeper Scripture study and community experiences.

With Kelley Mathews, Sue has coauthored *New Doors in Ministry to Women: A Fresh Model for Transforming Your Church, Campus, or Mission Field*; *Women's Retreats: A Creative Planning Guide*; and *Leading Women Who Wound: Strategies for an Effective Ministry*. Sue and Kelley joined with Henry Rogers to coauthor *Mixed Ministry: Working Together as Brothers and Sisters in an Oversexed Society*. Her newest book, coauthored with Barbara Neumann, *Organic Mentoring: A Mentor's Guide to Relationships with Next Generation Women*, explores the new values, preferences, and problems of the next generation and shows mentors how to avoid potential land mines and how to mentor successfully.

Sue has a doctor of ministry degree from Gordon-Conwell Theological Seminary in Boston and a master's in Bible from Dallas Theological Seminary. With Dr. Joye Baker, she oversees the Dallas Theological Seminary doctor of ministry degree in Christian education with a women-in-ministry emphasis.

Sue has been married to David over forty-five years. They have two married daughters, Heather and Rachel, and five grandchildren. David is a retired CAD applications engineer, a lay prison chaplain and founder of their church's prison ministry, and now a DTS student. Sue loves fine chocolates and exotic coffees, romping with her grandchildren, aquasize, and taking walks with David and her two West Highland terriers, Wallace and Emma Jane.